here & now

LIVING THE BEATITUDES IN TODAY'S WORLD

here & now

LIVING THE BEATITUDES IN TODAY'S WORLD

Rob Frost

See back of book for list of National Distributors.

Unless otherwise indicated, all Scripture references are from the Holy Bible: New
International Version (NIV), copyright © 1973, 1978, 1984 by the International Bible
Society.

Concept development, editing, design and production by CWR.
Front cover image: Chris Sands at Indigo Design.
Internal images: Brand X Pictures, Corbis Images, Digital Stock, Digital Vision,
image100, PhotoAlto, PhotoDisc, Stockbyte, Michael Kelley at Stone.
Printed in Croatia by Zrinski.

ISBN 1-85345-236-X

Contents

Acknowledgements

With thanks to Meryl Smith and Camille Troughton for help with compiling and typing the material.

Special thanks to the Here & Now production team involved with putting together the musical of the same name.

Thanks also to two doctors who helped me during ill health whilst writing this book – Dr Field and Dr Varney.

Introduction

The Beatitudes are found in Matthew 5 verses 3–10. They have always been very important to me. I remember learning them in Sunday School for a "Scripture" exam and proudly reciting them to my mother.

I remember reading them in Greek at Manchester University and pondering their meaning in an academic setting. I think, to be honest, that I was more intent on achieving a good exam grade than receiving some kind of spiritual revelation!

I asked Lady Diana to read them on a national television programme at the height of the Troubles in Northern Ireland. I gazed out over the squads of armed soldiers lying in the bushes all around us as she read, "Blessed are the peacemakers ..."

I've expounded them on convention platforms and preached them in village chapels. Again and again I've wondered at their poetry and marvelled at their meaning.

But I've never struggled with the Beatitudes as I have recently. The production team working on the musical, *Here & Now* was trying to write a two-hour show based on the Beatitudes.

The more we talked, however, the more confused we became until, at last, we gave up in desperation! When we moved onto the rather easier sections of the Sermon on the Mount the creativity flowed more easily.

When the pressure was off I went back to look at these simple phrases of Jesus for myself. I had only one question: Did Jesus intend the Beatitudes for the whole of society, or were they a personal challenge for Christians like me?

When I began to explore the Beatitudes as a personal agenda for my own life I felt a surge of power shoot through each phrase. The words challenged me to the core and gave me a completely new agenda. This book comes out of that experience.

Once I had encountered the true meaning of the Beatitudes for me, the rest of the Sermon on the Mount made perfect sense. I came to believe that this is the foundation for Christian discipleship.

I fully intended to write a commentary and to explain them in lucid theological terms. But when I started down that track the spark was quickly gone.

So this small book, *Here & Now*, is a personal journey through the Beatitudes. A poem, a meditation, a testimony. It's a pilgrimage that I welcome you to share.

1

Blessed are the poor in spirit, for theirs is the kingdom of heaven

Many of us are condemned by these kind words of Jesus.

We are condemned because we will not admit that we are poor in spirit.

We are condemned because poverty of spirit doesn't feature in the pressing agendas of our busy lives.

For without this recognition of spiritual poverty we condemn ourselves to days of self-delusion. To years of self-satisfaction. To a lifetime of spiritual bankruptcy. We are like paupers living in make-believe palaces.

Without this understanding of the deepest of all our needs, we can make no progress in the Christian life. For it is this recognition of our spiritual poverty which is the driving force for personal growth. The motivation which will propel us towards genuine holiness. The engine which empowers our journey to God.

Poverty of spirit is a poverty which we can never afford to be rid of. For, once we lose it, we lose reality. We have exchanged the changeless for the changing. The permanent for the transient. Truth for a lie.

So, at the start of this desert journey, we begin with a time of painful self-examination.

"Am I so wedded to the transient passing things of this life that I have divorced myself from the spiritual?"

"Is my life so focused on the things that I can see, touch, feel, buy, acquire, possess, own ... that I can no longer see the things which are eternal, invisible, immortal, everlasting or Spirit born?"

"Am I condemned by my poverty of spirit?"

THE FIRST PRAYER

Jesus looked down from the sacred hill. "Blessed. Favoured. Fortunate. Lucky," He said, are you who look into your heart and who face up to your spiritual bankruptcy. For when you truly comprehend your grinding poverty of spirit you'll want to seek out a different path. Search out a new way. Take a new road that will lead to spiritual wealth.

Following this new direction does not mean checking into your local monastery and devoting yourself to an eighteen-hour prayer vigil.

Nor does it lead to filling your life with the latest New Age gimmicks of meditation or mysticism.

Nor does it give you the right to assume an air of piety which will make you boring to know and unbearable to live with.

No. The first footstep on this pathway begins with a simple prayer.

"Lord Jesus, open my eyes that I might see."

It is a prayer that can be prayed in the most horrendous traffic jam. The most boring committee. The most arduous housework. The most challenging project. The most stressful decision.

It is a **prayer** that can be prayed at the liveliest party. Watching the most **sublime sunset**. Enfolded in the most loving **embrace**. Savouring the most **hallowed memory**. Tasting the most delicious dinner. Relaxing on the most **idyllic beach**.

This prayer is the dawning of reality. Less of me and more of God. A personal admission of spiritual poverty. And so I turn from self to God and pray.

"Lord Jesus, open my eyes that I might see."

THE FIRST LANDMARK

"Blessed. Favoured. Fortunate. Lucky," says Jesus, are those of you who are prepared to seek this pauper's path.

You have become hungry for Him. Hungry for His presence; His life; His love; His very being. In desiring Him you have recognised your own poverty and moved beyond it into the riches of His all-sufficiency.

Some say that this poverty of spirit only resides with the poor. Yet I have seen poor people with no understanding of it.

Others say that it cannot reside among the rich, but I have met it among them.

Some say that this poverty only comes when we have nothing, but I have seen those with nothing who lack it still.

Some say it cannot be found among those who have everything, but I have seen it there – when they have begun to regard everything as nothing.

The starting point of our journey, then, is a new hunger for God. A new admission of our poverty. A new desire for Him.

It doesn't come in a spiritual package of mantras or prayer books, of ritualistic routines or of worship rites.

It comes from my heart.

"Lord, open my eyes that I might see."

A daily quest for God in the everyday. An openness. A searching. A simple trust that in asking, I will receive; in seeking, I will find; in knocking, the door will be opened to me. It comes when I admit to Him ...

"Lord, I am poor in spirit."

The first marker on my journey, then, is a frank admission.

Lord. I'm broke. I'm bankrupt. I'm all washed up. I'm finished. I'm desperate. I'm hungry. I'm deep in need.

THE FIRST BLESSING

This small beginning is all-significant.

It is a turning from self-sufficiency to God-sufficiency. From me to Him. For when I long for more of God He meets me where I am.

And when I turn from self to Him I move from personal poverty of spirit to eternal wealth. From spiritual bankruptcy to divine plenty.

This hunger, then, brings the first blessing: In longing for more of God I have found His heaven here on earth. When I knocked, the door was opened. When I asked, I received. When I sought, I found. Unexpectedly, I have discovered the gold dust of heaven in the cobweb corners of ordinary life.

This heaven belongs to those who recognise their poverty. Who are **hungry for more**. Who search out **God stuff** among all the other stuff. Poor as they are, they have claimed a stake in the territory of God's **incalculable riches**.

The poor in spirit are the needy ones who reach up to heaven and pull down daily handfuls of its glory.

They are the little ones who feebly reach out to God and feel His hands take theirs with a never-loosening grip.

They are the broken ones who push through the darkness of their bleak experiences to let in heaven's light.

The poor in spirit have unexpectedly found the kingdom of heaven right where they are!

This, perhaps, is the greatest mystery of all. That this paradise; this everlasting country; this place without tears; this bliss of eternal love; this presence of the living God; this kingdom of heaven – belongs to us – here and now!

Blessed are the poor in spirit, for theirs is the kingdom of heaven

This kingdom is ours! It begins here and it starts now and it lasts for ever. And all we ever needed to do was to ask, to seek, to knock – so that the door to it could be opened wide!

This kingdom bursts into my consciousness when I feel I've let go of Him – but sense His everlasting grip.

This kingdom comes when I can't accept myself ... but hear His whispered promise, "You are accepted ... welcome."

This kingdom comes when I feel my human weakness – but am infused afresh with His surpassing strength.

This kingdom comes when the dark days of my past are filled with His redemptive light.

It comes in His all-sufficiency for my needs today.

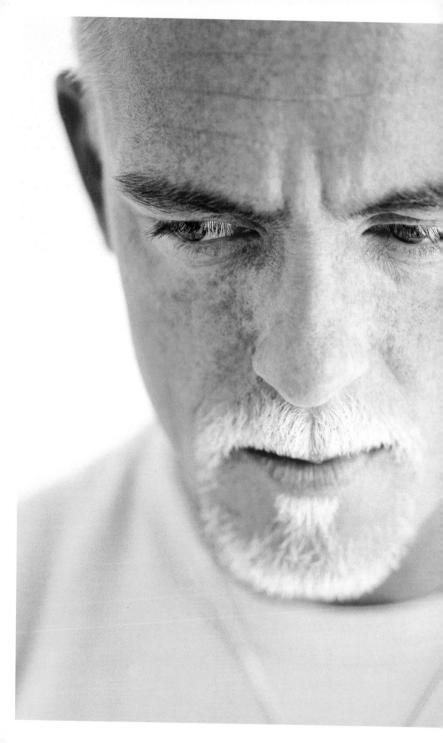

2

Blessed are those who mourn, for they will be comforted

RETRACING MY STEPS

Jesus gazed out across the harsh desert plains before Him. He spoke from the heights of the sacred hill as the cool breeze brushed His face. The desert sun was sinking behind the hills and it cast long shadows across the well-worn pilgrim track which led up from the valley below.

Jesus was calling them to discover a difficult kind of blessedness. A blessedness only to be found through painful introspection, through lament for what has been. The blessing of the lessons that are learned from the hilltop of hindsight. The blessing of mourning for what was and what might have been.

His was a message which has been lost to many of us today. His words have been blown away like footprints in the desert sand. A powerful message, eroded by the winds of time. Yet the value of this retrospective view is as great today as ever.

Sadly, many of us have never learned the benefits of mourning, nor found the gift of sombre introspection. Rather, we have loaded our diaries with hasty plans to fill tomorrow. We've scheduled ourselves into the empty security of a never-ending round of busy days.

We've made plans for what will be, preferring the excitement of a clean-sheet future to facing up to the harsh realities of yesterday. We are the generation which lives for what will be, but with no understanding of what has gone before.

We measure ourselves against those of lesser stature. Judge our performance against the mediocre reputations of our peers. Congratulate ourselves on a job well done.

We look back and mark out our worldly achievements like trophies on display or we single out our passing moments of temporal glory. We recall the day when applause rang loud for us and when we tasted fame.

We commend ourselves for a life well lived. Reward ourselves because we made the best of what we had. A kind of personal "This is your life" edited to prove that our journey wasn't all a waste of time. But, sadly, it's all just an escape from how we've really lived.

It's true that each of us has travelled a different journey to this point in time; been shaped by different influences; moulded by different experiences; fashioned by different relationships.

Each of us could make a great defence for all we've done, citing **"circumstances beyond our control"** as the excuse for what we've become. But, as we stand in this high place of the **here and now** and look back across the years we've travelled, there is much we **need to face**.

This is the saved space in which we must face up to yesterday. This view of the past can become our teacher in the here and now and our guide towards a new tomorrow.

And so I look back down the winding road of memory and find that there is much for me to learn. Retracing my steps down the long track of personal experience, I begin to see what's really true and see how I've failed Him at last. A journey of honest introspection, with Jesus as my Guide.

THE KIND GUIDE

But this Saviour Guide is no "ghost of Christmas past". He's not here to haunt me with the failures of yesterday. He is no ugly spectre come to frighten or condemn me.

No, this is a kinder Guide whose grace has already covered a multitude of sins. A Saviour Guide who's come to redeem my past, not to use it as evidence against me.

This is a **friendly Guide** who doesn't come in **judgment** but with a **love** for me far deeper than I know. He invites me to **gaze back down** the desert track I've travelled and to see the rich panoply of **experiences** spread out across my **plains of memory**.

He takes my hand to walk me through the fragile web of past relationships and to see again the tangles that my life has wrought. He shows me things that I had conveniently erased from memory.

He takes my hand to guide me through the fragile web.

This mourning that I feel, then, is not for the past itself. Not a bereavement for the loss of faces long gone nor for distant friends in faraway places. This mourning is not a sense of grief for the memories I've forgotten, nor the lost fragments of my childhood past.

No, this is a mourning for my life. A lament for what I have become.

THE ROAD TO REALITY

If I do not take this retrospective journey I will live on in the fantasy world of unreality. I'll live a lie, protected by the figment of my own cosmetically-improved imagination. I'll continue touching up my past in the vain hope of making it more acceptable today.

If I don't go backwards down the years with my tender Guide, I'll continue to live a fairytale. I'll simply edit out those parts of my past story which have embarrassed me; spin-doctoring my life into something more appealing. And all this in the vain hope that I may come to like myself and live more easily with my past.

But this is not reality. No, **reality comes** when I take His hand and walk back down the years. It comes in **understanding** that, even at my very best I was never really good enough.

It's fully facing the truth that, despite my self-congratulation, I have failed to be what He had hoped I'd be. It's knowing that even when I chose the higher cause my motives were

mixed and my ambitions driven by a darker force.

Reality is a journey back to look into the faces of the ones I've hurt. It's having Him point out the well-marked signs I missed along the way. It's understanding how things could have been if only I had gone His way.

Reality is what's written on the sad, hurting faces of those I passed by on the other side. Reality is forgotten promises, selfish relationships, well-shaped lies.

Reality is seeing how I've changed. Recognising how the long years of self-seeking have tarnished me. How the faces of my public image have masked my true identity.

Reality is grieving over the high ideals of youth now levelled by the complex compromises of a busy life. Understanding how the bright trusting faith of a new believer grew shabby, polluted by a dirty world.

Reality is seeing myself as I really am, not as I would like to be seen. Seeing me as He sees me, with all His omniscient insight of the years and His understanding of who I really am.

At last I see myself as a shadow of what I could have been. I see the death of everything I used to boast about. For the truth is, my best was never good enough and my past was not what I have cracked it up to be.

THE PLACE OF TRUTH

This, then, is where the mourning starts. My gentle Guide has brought me to the place of truth and the pain of it unplugs the wellspring of my tears. It drives me to my knees.

Here, from this vantage place of hindsight, a cloud of sadness envelops me. And the only word I have is "Sorry".

And even as the word is spoken this **cloud of desolation** slowly lifts. The **bright beams** of a new dawn are breaking through. I hear His word of grace and feel His **warm embrace**. I am forgiven, even for all my past.

The sun rises over the long road ahead and I see a land of opportunity stretching out towards the far horizon. And there is hope now.

I know for sure that the past is His and His alone and that the future brings a new beginning. I go forward from this new place of reality to forge a new tomorrow. I have found what He promised ...

> Blessed are those who mourn,
> for they will be comforted.

And from here to eternity I will live a different life.

3

Blessed are the meek, for they will inherit the earth

MY VIEW

For most of us, our view of the world is framed by our ambitions, filtered by our aspirations, focused by our heart's desires.

We look out through the lens of our hopes and dreams and choose the perspective that pleases us most. We can choose to see the world as a place to be conquered or as a people to be served.

It's a landscape to be possessed or loved ones to be liberated. A country to be ruled or a community to be cared for. Ultimately, we come to see the world either as something which belongs to us or as something which belongs to God.

But here, on the Mount of Beatitudes, there is a different view. This high vantage point gives me the right perspective. But, sadly, there are millions who travel the plains of life's long journey but who never stop to see things from this angle.

This is the high place where I come to seek answers for my

biggest questions. What has it been about, my journey? A chance to collect more assets on the way? Pile up possessions on the handcart? Get more security by burying treasure in the ground?

What has it been about, my journey?

Why did I jump the queue, rip off the innocent, falsify the scales, give short change?

Why did I spend the journey grabbing bargains while missing the view along the way?

Why was I so preoccupied with get instead of give? Me instead of them? More instead of less?

What has my life been for?

Placed in the scales of eternity, weighed in the balance of perfect love, calibrated in the justice of judgment: How do I measure up?

These are the questions for those who would be meek.

TEMPTATION VIEW

There are many views from a hilltop. Many emotions to be stirred, many lessons learned.

You can stand on a high hill and crown yourself the king of all you see. The lofty structures of power lie dwarfed in miniature at your feet.

The **hierarchies** of men are diminished to **ant-like proportions** in the **lofty perspective** of this highest height.

The devil once showed Jesus a view like this. He took Him, hungry and tired, from His forty days of wilderness and showed Him the tempter's view. A view from the very edge.

And there, from that tall place of temptation, Jesus gazed out on the wonders of the world. He saw the passing civilisations paraded in their splendour. He watched as the majestic kings of earth bowed in salute. He tasted the wonders of inestimable wealth and savoured the richness of the finest global culture.

There was everything, spread out before Him, and all He had to do was ask. There was the very best, arranged in packages like priceless items at an auction house, and all He had to do was nod His bid of acquiescence.

Here were the finest things on earth spread out before Him and He only need sign His name. Serve Himself and, in so doing, serve the tempter sitting patiently before Him.

But in the choking crucible on the tempter's furnace He did not melt. His steely conviction was still stronger than the fires of hell. His iron will, white hot with anguish, stood unmelted yet. His firm resolve, though licked by flames of deadly evil, was still unbroken.

And in that scorching moment He said, "No," and this rejection of things carnal, temporal and transient, echoed down the rest of history. For in that moment He chose **meekness** over **majesty**. **Obedience** over **obeisance**. **Sacrifice** over **self**. **Personhood** over **possession**.

And in that moment He rejected everything – and inherited the lot.

THE VIEW OF THE MEEK

"Blessed. Favoured. Fortunate. Lucky," says Jesus, are you who discover the same joy. You've found the strength to turn your back on what the world can offer and choose a meeker path. And, in so doing, you follow in the footsteps of the One who's gone before.

Born in a borrowed stable, buried in a borrowed tomb. No place to lay His head. No mighty stallion carried Him into Jerusalem, just a simple donkey bore Him along the road to death.

His seamless garment was the winner's prize in a gambling game. The Man with nothing, yet with everything. The King of the universe had become the Servant of them all. He who lost the lot on Friday had won it all back by Sunday.

"Blessed are the meek," He said. A blessedness He fought for on the Mount of Temptation and a blessedness He imparted on the Mount of Beatitudes. A blessedness which brings joy in abundance.

They say that this world belongs to the powerful. The ones who buy and sell. Who build up or pull down. Create or destroy. Make or break. But Jesus proved that in reality it all belongs to the meek.

For the really special things are not for sale. There is no market value on serving others. No scale for calculating the worth of him who shares. There is no price on love.

> Blessed are the meek,
> for they will inherit the earth.

But aren't these words a contradiction?

The meek ... with everything?

The losers ... win all?

The people who give ... get the lot?

The ones who demanded least ... get most?

**Those who pushed their way to the back ...
end up at the front?**

**The little ones who considered themselves last ...
finally come first?**

"Blessed. Favoured. Fortunate. Lucky," says Jesus, are the meek.

They have invested their lives in things more worthwhile than stocks, more valuable than money, more important than stuff.
And in serving this greater cause it has cost them much but has brought an abundance of good things on the way.

THE BEST VIEW

And so, from this high vantage point, I pause to take in the view. I see the world spread out like a banquet. The finest things on earth displayed before me. And then His words ring round the rock hard caverns of the hilltop range.

> Blessed are the meek,
> For they will inherit the earth.

For His topsy-turvy view of things has set all human values on their head.

For those of us who devote ourselves to money will never discover its true value.

And those who chase endlessly after success will never savour its true flavour.

And those who are consumed with getting more will never have the time to appreciate what they already have.

But if we "seek first his kingdom and his righteousness", we live a different life. Our treasure is in heaven. Our riches lie in His kingdom. Our worth is in the love of God.

We won't worry about tomorrow, for God will provide.

By living life from this perspective we've become **"earth inheritors"**: the people who've discovered that true life is discovered in meekness **here and now**.

We've become Christ's little ones who have found heaven on earth today and who look forward to a new heaven and a new earth at the end of time itself.

We've become the ones who live a life of meekness rather than a life of majesty. Who've discovered obedience over obeisance. Sacrifice over self. Personhood over possession.

So, climb the steep hill of the Beatitudes again.

And find the high place where old ambitions are laid to rest and where other dreams rise fresh with the new dawn.

And from this high vantage point of the here and now discover again that you want to serve God, and God alone.

4

Blessed are they
who hunger and thirst
for righteousness,
for they will be filled

THE THIRST OF THE DESERT

Jesus stood on the holy hill and looked over the desert plain before Him. Endless miles of wilderness stretched out toward the far horizon. Barren rocks, deep canyons, windswept plains, dusty paths. A harsh and arid land.

The view from this side of the hilltop was not of lush oasis, green-grassed pasture or a source of springs. No, this was a land of hunger and a country of thirst. A place where desert travellers knew the parched pain of dehydration.

"Blessed. Favoured. Fortunate," said Jesus, are those who are really thirsty. Lucky are those of you who look for righteousness with all the desperation of a hungry traveller who looks for food on the desert plain.

This kind of hunger and thirst will ensure that your focus is fixed, your attention undivided. You will journey single-mindedly for goodness in the desolation of an evil world.

From this high vantage point Jesus could see that it was not rules which kept the weary travellers moving when the sun was sinking low. From this lookout He knew it wasn't regulations which kept the pilgrims pressing onward as the moon rose high.

No. It was thirst which drove men upwards when the road was steep and the going hard. It was the pain of hunger which spurred the weary travellers on ... long after the desire for everything else had gone. "Blessed", then, are the ones who have this thirsty need for righteousness.

It was thirst which drove men upwards when the road was steep and the going hard.

MAN-MADE RIGHTEOUSNESS

The righteousness of which Jesus spoke, however, was not the man-made legalism popular in His day. This Pharisaic kind of righteousness was more a calorie-controlled snack than a banquet of compassion.

The righteousness of His time was like a gastronomical delight. A diverse menu of legalistic delicacies which food experts could relish for their flavour. But it didn't feed hungry souls.

The righteousness of His time was like the **sniff of a wine's bouquet** rather than **gushing water** for a parched throat. A fine list of good deeds to be swilled across the palate and spat out in silver salvers mouthful by mouthful. Not a **spring of living water** for **thirsty people**.

The righteousness-reviewers savoured the flavours of acceptable behaviour, compared the vintage of this deed to the maturity of another. Sampled morsels of goodness and graded them by degree of flavour.

They held tastings of legal interpretations. Compared recipes on the way to live. Gave star ratings to each other's reputations. Became gluttons for fine restaurants, but lacked any taste for the food itself.

In this view from the holy hill, however, Jesus could see that the high peaks of man-made righteousness were as nothing. These lofty human aspirations of do-gooders were of no lasting value. He despised their self-congratulatory forms of goodness and despaired of such ego-driven acts of kindness.

His view was a topsy-turvy view. He could see clearly that true righteousness is not a set of rules to obey, but a hunger to satisfy. Not a set of regulations to adhere to, but a thirst to quench.

True righteousness is not a set of rules to obey, but a hunger to satisfy.

TRUE RIGHTEOUSNESS

He taught, then, that true righteousness goes beyond the letter of the law. It can't be framed by fine words from legal minds. It's not imprisoned by the jargon of the courtroom or bound by the solicitor's red wax seal.

True righteousness goes beyond good reputations. It's more than not blotting your copybook. It's superior to a **clean image**. Greater than doing your **best**.

True righteousness is higher than normal standards. It defines anger as murder. Determines lust as adultery. Decides that a man's word is his bond. Demands that if someone strikes you on the right cheek, you offer the left also. Delights in loving enemies – whoever they may be.

True righteousness is like good fruit from a healthy tree, it's all delicious. Whichever branch you choose. Whichever piece you pick. Whichever part you taste. There's nothing rotten here, for everything is connected and all is nourished from the same pure root.

This kind of righteousness is not defined by rules and regulations. You don't discover it by living balanced codes of conduct. You don't adopt it by weighing acceptable behaviour in the scale of social norms. You don't live it by talking about it or demonstrate it by telling others how much good you've done.

No, this righteousness comes when you're hungry for it. A hunger that keeps you serving when the path is steep and the going tough. It satisfies the kind of thirst that keeps you loving, even when the way ahead seems impassable.

It's a righteousness driven by **hunger** and powered by **thirst**. It propels us **forward** when everything in the world would have us turn **back**. It drives us on **against the grain** of ordinary human behaviour and marks us out in **contrast** to the social standards of our day.

This righteousness is hard. It's tough. It's demanding. It's difficult. It can even be dangerous. And if you're not hungry or thirsty for it you'll never find it for yourself.

Blessed are they who hunger and thirst for righteousness, for they will be filled

True righteousness is like good fruit from a healthy tree.

SATISFIED AT LAST

"Blessed. Favoured. Fortunate. Lucky," says Jesus, are those who are really hungry for righteousness. They have the motivation to make a difference, the kind of drive which will keep them doing good when everyone else has long turned back.

"Blessed. Favoured. Fortunate. Lucky," says Jesus, are those who are really thirsty for righteousness. For this thirst gives you the power to love others, even when they don't love you. A thirst which makes you want to love your enemies as much as you love your friends.

I see now that I have done my best to obey the rules and tried to adhere to the regulations for long enough. I have done my best and failed. Adopted middle-class norms of behaviour instead of God's standards. Aimed at decency but missed the mark of holiness.

But now I have a hunger for something more significant. A heart's desire to live a life that's more than tidy. I want to out-perform the average.

This, then, is my **mountain-top moment**. The chance to stop and start again. An opportunity to take a **different path** driven only by a pure desire for good. To live a life so bound to His that I will want what He wants and **hunger and thirst** for what's on His heart.

Here and now, I want to be joined to Christ. I want my life to become His life. To be compassion exemplified. To know a righteousness that does not set me above the rest – but which sets the rest above me. I want His hunger for a better world and His thirst for a transformed society to become my own!

And so His appetite for goodness has becomes mine. And now I will desire what's best. His craving for goodness has come alive in me. Our desires have merged into a perfect quest for good. And I know that, through this transformation of who I am I will at last be fully satisfied.

A righteousness that does not set me above the rest – but which sets the rest above me.

5

Blessed are the merciful, for they will be shown mercy

APOCALYPSE VIEW

The view from the hilltop was spectacular. Lush fields, olive groves and the rippling waters of Galilee. But Jesus saw a different scene.

He looked beyond the boundary of human history and gazed out to the end of all things. He slowly surveyed the solemn scene. For there, beyond Him, He saw the vast empires of men lying in ruins across the plains of time.

The **fortunes** of the rich lay covered by the **sands of time**. The **grandiose plans** of ambitious leaders blew like scraps of paper across the **barren landscape**.

The finest accomplishments of famous men lay buried in the graveyards of ancient history. The philosophies of the greatest minds were piled up high, dusty and decaying in the desert air.

The shining reputations of the brilliant were stacked up high, slowly tarnished by the steady erosion of time. The purest reputations covered in dirt. The proudest achievements of the pioneers reduced to rubble.

And here, on this lowland of judgment, the profiles of the beautiful were dead and decomposing. The most popular of celebrities left all alone, deserted by the mob. Nothing stirred, save the eerie whine of the desert breeze of condemnation.

Jesus watched this **apocalyptic scene** and saw, from this hilltop of eternity, how little of **humanity's greatness** remained in the **aftermath of history**. The merciful judgment of God had revealed what was **hidden** and had measured falsehood with the yardstick of **perfect truth**.

And there, standing before Him, were the legions of the condemned. Shrouded by derision, covered by guilt, saturated by selfishness. Left with nothing to cover their shame but the anguish of regret and the rags of shame.

This was a dark view, indeed. This was the burial ground of history, where nothing remained save the dull ache of

memory. There was nought of lasting value here.

Left with nothing ... but the anguish of regret and the rags of shame.

THE PLAIN OF GRACE

Jesus turned away. His heart broken by such waste. His mind still full of what might have been. This was human tragedy on a grand scale.

He turned towards the other side of the mountain and fixed His gaze on a different view. Another lookout over the affairs of men, a vantage point where all could be clearly seen.

From this other lookout there was a brighter aspect. For here there was no vista of dereliction, but a panorama bright with daylight hope for the future of humankind.

This was the plain of grace. The plateau of justice where the relative greatness of men was levelled by the perfect wisdom of God. For here, man's status was not marked by his stature in human history but by the measure of his mercy alone.

At last the King spoke.

"I was **hungry** and you gave me something to **eat**."

The crowd grew restless.

"I was **thirsty** and you gave me something to **drink**."

They looked at one another, disbelieving.

"I was a **stranger** and you **invited me in**."

There was a murmur of incredulity.

"I needed **clothes** and you **clothed me**."

They were shaking their heads. Sceptical.

"I was **sick** and you **looked after me**."

"Lord, when ...?" shouted one.

"I was in **prison** and you **came to visit me**."

The crowd murmured "No" in disbelief.

And then the King's voice echoed from the hilltops.

"I tell you the truth, whatever you did for **one of the least** of these brothers of mine, **you did for me**."

The people fell silent. For, finally, they knew. It was mercy that had brought them through the fires of condemnation and grace that had brought them safe to the other side.

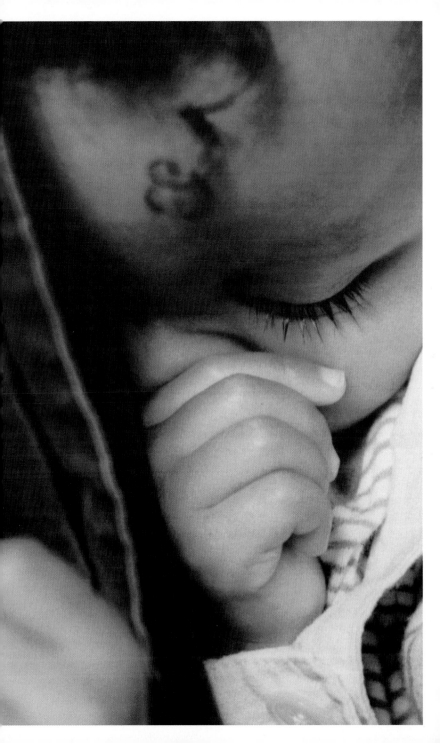

Man's status was not marked by his stature in human history but by the measure of his mercy alone.

Here they were then, the multitudes He called the "Blessed. Favoured. Fortunate. Lucky". The people who had lived for mercy above all else.

These were the little ones whose lives had exemplified the very character of God and whose deeds had outshone the brightest heroes of the human story.

This **army of the ordinary** were not robed in vestiges of honour as they stood before their King. They wore no **freshly-minted medals** sparkling in the morning sun. They could not boast of extraordinary greatness, for their goodness had **gone unnoticed** in the annals of human history.

No, these were the little ones. The ones who felt unworthy to be there at all. They knew their reputations could make no claim against the ravages of time and they stood in awkward silence awaiting the revelation of God's perfect justice at the end of everything.

JUDGMENT DAY

Two views from a hilltop. Two sides of future story. Two glimpses of eternity from before the end of time. This spectacular view from the hilltop of history helps me to see myself in the perspective of eternity. A chance to see things as they really are.

And so I spread my life out before me, like fading photos from an old shoe-box. I reach out for my past, like an old diary, and open up the faded pages. I clean off long-lost memories which lie gathering dust. I try, at last, to unravel the jumble of relationships that I'd promised would one day be set in order.

I fold up my differing roles, like old dressing-up clothes spilling out of a rusty trunk. And in this personal judgment day I see the reality of the person I've become. So many opportunities for kindness lost for good. So many chances to love missed along the way. So many hurting people that remained ignored. Simple deeds that would have made things better remain left undone.

For out of all my life's priorities I had overlooked the most important one of all. To be **merciful, compassionate, gracious** and **kind**. To do the very things which would survive the fire of judgment day.

Perhaps, in the theological gamesmanship I've played, I've missed the potency of this simple truth. Maybe, while I was fixing my life on winning the world, I overlooked mercy and lost my soul.

Mercy is the hallmark of the kingdom people. Mercy, the characteristic of those who really belong. Mercy is the guarantee of human authenticity. Mercy, the sign of the living God.

How, then, could I have ever expected mercy if it had always been a stranger to me? How could I have anticipated it, if I had never known it in my life? Watched for it, if I didn't know what it looked like? Waited for it, without knowing what to expect?

As I look out over the dark shadows of the plain of judgment, I see the lost years of my life eaten away with self. The human prizes for which I competed, now only fit for scrap. My most important hopes, now relegated to the faded dreams of yesterday. A hard-lived life that lacked mercy.

But from this holy hilltop I see a **brighter future**.
A line of tomorrows cast in a different light. A life made
up of mercy. A chance to **change the world**
I meet.

And in this merciful new beginning I discover something
great: That in the sharing of mercy with the hurting ones
along the way, this strange grace rebounds to meet me –
like some boomerang of kindness. Mercy has found me at
last. Mercy has come home to rest.

Jesus smiles at me from the hilltop of judgment. Perhaps
I've learnt at last that ...

> Blessed are the merciful,
> for they will be shown mercy.

**Mercy is the guarantee of human
authenticity ... the sign of the living
presence of God.**

6

Blessed are the pure in heart, for they will see God

BLIND LEADING THE BLIND

Jesus looked down from the mountain's edge, and gazed at the vast number of pilgrims who were travelling across the plain below. His view from the mountain was a clear view and from this aspect He could see their progress perfectly.

It was a view unimpeded by bright city lights. Unobstructed by the tall vanities of a fallen age. This perfect panorama was not blocked by prejudice nor cut short by intolerance. It was a view which revealed the things which are hidden and it exposed the mixed motives which drove so many of them on.

Jesus looked down from this high vantage point and gazed deep into the hearts of men. He looked beyond the fine cut of wealthy robes and past the threadbare rags of the poor. He saw beyond the masquerading masks of make-up and the cold cosmetic of constructed conceit.

His gaze penetrated beyond a skin-deep perspective. His sight was all-embracing. His view was like none other. It was a view from a different place. For from this high ledge of clarity He saw into the hidden caverns of each mind and penetrated the darkest depths of every personality.

His insight reached past their years of self-sufficiency and extended beyond their lifetimes of deceit. His gaze was never diverted by the fine manners of the proud nor deflected by the rude obscenities of the ignorant. His laser vision peeled away the layers of complex personality and viewed the hearts of men in fine focus.

All was **revealed** in His stilled concentration in this sacred place. His loving look cut through the vanities of noble deeds and showed the emptiness within. His **penetrating sight** saw through ostentatious acts of goodness to reveal **cold hearts** devoid of compassion.

His view looked deep into the hearts of men. Hearts attacked by hatred. Stilled by malice. Frozen by self. Dead. Impure. Compromised. Defiled. Unworthy.

He saw behind high walls of piety and uncovered lives of religious duty thickly coated by the gloss of vainglory. His look went beyond broad smiles and revealed dark secrets. He saw the truth in each of us.

He saw the truth in each of us.

It was little wonder, then, that some of the pilgrims journeying towards Him were meandering aimlessly along the desert plain. They walked around in circles without recognising they were passing the point from which they'd already come.

Their journey, while continuing without end, never reached its destination. They never caught a glimpse of God. They imagined they were making progress but they never advanced towards their goal.

They were blind travellers. Groping despondently to find the way – but never seeing. Their journey had taken them to the furthest reaches of the planet but they were no closer to God's finishing line than when they first began. They had seen it all, save what they sought to see – a clear view of God.

And at the head of this long procession going nowhere were the unseeing guides. The blind leading the blind. Lost leaders in a wilderness of disbelief. Heading off in all directions save the right one.

These lost leaders were constantly confusing everyone with their pious instructions. Expecting standards which they couldn't reach themselves. Laying burdens on others which they refused to carry personally. They were confused about the way ahead and constantly confusing others in the process.

LIVING IN THE FOG

"Blessed. Favoured. Fortunate. Lucky," says Jesus, "are the pure in heart." They have travelled wisely. They have invested their energy in something more than empty religion.

They have given time to something more than reputation. Spent themselves on something more than the fading glory of human honour. Sought a virtue beyond the gaze of men. They have become pure in heart and, as a result, they have seen God.

And so I stop dead in my tracks on my journey across the dusty plain. I sense the fog of my impurity on every side and feel His watchful eye resting on me. No word is spoken, but I kneel in speechless humiliation at my stupidity.

His gaze sees through my smoke screen of good works and the camouflage of self-made righteousness. He looks into my heart. I see at last that the journey I have travelled was mistaken.

I'd been living as if He judged by my **appearances** and not by my **heart**. I had travelled in the hope that I might **discover Him**, but now I know it's asking Him to **reveal Himself** to me.

Here, as a stalled pilgrim, I am reduced to tears. My strong defences lie breached. My false pretences shown up for what they really are. My religion deconstructed by a look. My life-history uncovered in the blink of an eye. I am convicted. Broken. Humbled. Real before my God.

He looks into my heart.

SEEING GOD

And so, at last, I come to recognise the folly of my journey. The self-made salvation awarded to myself lies broken and in pieces. My religious practice lies wrecked and written off and ready for the scrap heap.

The **crumbs of comfort** that I've offered now look stale. My glittering goodness looks **tarnished in the midday sun**. And round the caverns of the mountain His voice rings out the **awful truth**.

Blessed are the pure in heart,
for they will see God.

And in this place of tears I recognise at last, that God is not to be found, like some player in a cosmic game of hide-and-seek. God is not to be discovered, like some formula in the science lab. God is not dug up, like some artefact uncovered by the archaeologist's trowel. God is not located, like treasure on a desert island.

No, God reveals Himself to the pure in heart.

The fog of my self-centredness slowly lifts as I turn from self to Him in the warmth of His accepting love. The mist of sin is burnt away by the radiance of His holy fire.

In this yielding of the inner part of who I am I sense the birth of purity. In bowing down to God and yielding the inner core of who I am I sense the first warm rays of holiness.

And so I finally reach the mountain and understand at last that God reveals Himself to whom He chooses. The people who find Him aren't selected because of power or wealth or fame. No, He simply chooses the pure in heart … for they are most like Him.

And finally it all makes sense. A holy God meets with holy people. I come afresh to live that life and to see my God. I come at last to know that blessed are the pure in heart.

A holy God meets with holy people.

7

Blessed are the peacemakers, for they will be called sons of God

THE MENAGERIE OF WAR

Jesus looked down from the holy hill and saw the peaceful waters of Galilee. Beyond the further shore lay the dark outline of the Golan Heights and above them tall black clouds of smoke were ascending into the clear sky.

Slowly rising through the shimmering heat came the distant clamour of endless suffering. Men communicating at cross-purposes. Angry voices raised in bitter conflict. Emotive calls to battle. Orders shouted in blind disobedience to God.

A growing crescendo of discord, until finally came the shrill echo of bloody screams. Pain was everywhere, and the Galilean waters were turning crimson with blood.

And as He looked across the space of time towards the coming generations, He saw the rising potential of mass destruction. And He heard the distant echo of gunfire resounding down the centuries towards Him.

Distant bombing disturbed the still, waters of the Galilee. He looked beyond the placid hills and far into the future. And His eye followed the long white vapour trails of fighter planes criss-crossing the bright heavens of a distant age.

He saw with horror how the menagerie of war was improving with the years, but the venom at the heart of it was just the same. And, wherever it began, it began in simplicity.

Rumours of discontent were whispered in Roman drinking houses. **Emotions** became stirred in Dickensian coffee shops. Malicious **gossip** spread through Victorian tea-rooms. People in cold war isolation were **separated** by an iron curtain of silence.

And soon the same dark forces were spreading electronically at the speed of light. Telegrams spreading venom. Vicious accusation communicated instantly by email. Insidious text messages destroying long-established relationships. Voicemail plots echoing back and forth across the planet. Websites calling for revenge. Radio phone-ins stoking public anger.

Slowly, but irrevocably, in every age, the same cycle was repeated. Disquiet growing into disagreement and dis-

agreement to disputation. Disrespect becoming dissent. Distortion turning to dissension. Disunity driving the world's agenda. Until at last, in every age, true love had disappeared.

And then came fighting. Swords or spitfires, cannons or carpet bombs, muskets or missiles – these were the tools of hatred, the apparatus of enmity, the machinery of conflict. The things that men used when words failed them.

He fell to the ground with the weight of it. The enormity of the suffering. The endless agony of the bleeding wounds. The ceaseless misery of destruction. The wicked cruelty of undeserved torture. The never-ending inhumanity made acceptable by an unquenchable thirst for victory.

The distant echo of gunfire resounding across the centuries.

SONS OF GOD

"Blessed are the peacemakers," He shouted.

But above the roar of war most could not hear His voice.

"The peacemakers are My brothers and sisters, they are family to Me, they belong to My kingdom ... they are truly the sons of God."

He taught that peacemaking is not an activity reserved for politicians, not preserved exclusively for ambassadors, not solely the domain of the United Nations.

For peacemaking is not about treaties or alliances, bonds or pacts. Nor does it start with opposing generals signing documents of cease-fire.

No, there are vacancies for everyday peacemakers everywhere:

Where marriage partners turn their backs towards each other as the sun goes down on their anger.

Where people who live next door to each other issue writs rather than invitations.

Where workers prefer anger to arbitration or employers choose conflict over conciliation.

Where human relationships break down.

Where conflict between human beings becomes unresolvable.

Where people stop talking to one another.

Where backs are turned against the "opposition".

Where differences between individuals are irreconcilable.

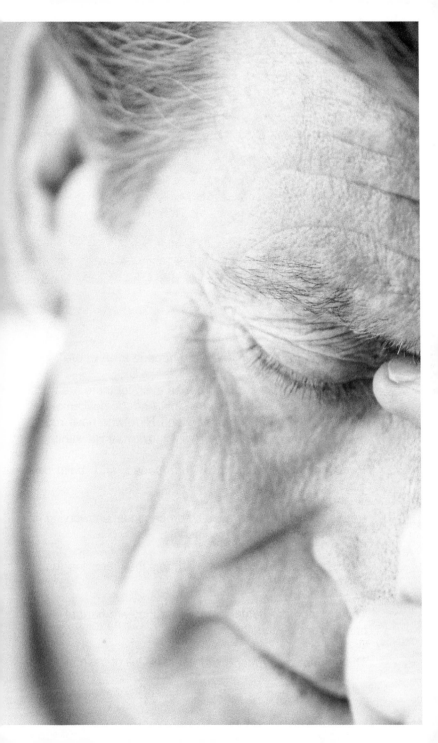

Where those who once walked together now go their separate ways.

Yes. Everyday peacemakers are needed everywhere.

And we need them now more than ever, for there are wars and rumours of wars on every side. And the peacemakers are the ones who have understood Him, who have made sense of His Word and who really know what He wants.

Peacemakers break down barricades and build up dialogue.

Peacemakers are unswayed by propaganda, unswerving in obedience, unimpressed by medals.

Peacemakers do not demolish for they are too busy building.

They do not tear humanity apart for they are hard at work bringing people together.

They do not root up for their hands are full of fresh seed.

Peacemaking demands courage.

They refuse to buy the party line. They question the propaganda of one side and disbelieve the press releases of the "other". Peacemakers live in a "no-man's-land" where neither side supports them.

This is the lonely place of the peacemaker.

For whenever you try to believe the best about people,
stem the tide of gossip,
refuse to join the buzz of whispered character
assassination, stay neutral,
hold hands across the borders of confrontation …
you will be hated. A traitor to all except your God.

Where men shout angry words at each other
through megaphones of hatred few will hear you.

Where voices are raised in violent conflict no one will
want to listen to your words of love.

Where stonewall silence separates people you won't

want to be the first to speak.

Where men shout an "eye for an eye" you may be blinded by their united hatred.

But still – blessed are the peacemakers.

THE PEACEMAKER IN YOU

So where does it come from, this peacemaker in you?

From some qualification in negotiation? From some understanding of legal rights? From some skill-base acquired in evening class? From a new awareness of the psychology of conflict?

No. Peacemakers carry that unique gene which comes straight from God. For the Person who is Three in One is reconciliation personified. This Father, Son and Holy Spirit models perfect harmony.

This Trinity trust is a trust which recognises uniqueness but enjoys unity. It celebrates otherness while maintaining togetherness. It's separate yet one. Different but the same.

It's this divine spark of reconciling love from the very heart of God which makes a peacemaker. True peacemakers carry the reconciling wounds of God wherever they go. They have left self behind and carry the cross of sacrifice. They are moulded by love. Shaped by compassion. Driven by a gospel of new beginnings. Their lives are full of grace.

Peacemakers aren't trained, they're **inspired**. They're not qualified, they're empowered. They're not obeying orders, they're **driven by a vision**. They're not following an agenda, they're living a life.

The life of a peacemaker is a life whose source is in God and whose inspiration is a cross. The peacemaker's commitment is fuelled by a power greater than his own, the power of the Holy Spirit.

For the peacemaker, all of life is a celebration of Jesus' life. For He is the Reconciler. The Bringer together. The Redeemer of human brokenness. The One who died on a cross with arms open wide. Whose dying breath carried the word "FORGIVE". Bleeding love personified.

The life of a peacemaker doesn't start at a place of conflict. It starts at a cross.

It doesn't begin with kind words and calm sentiments. It starts with Calvary's agony.

It's not something from you, it's something from Him.

The strength of the peacemaker comes from knowing you are **accepted**. Believing you are **forgiven**. Knowing the healing bliss of entering **Divine Love**.

Peacemaking starts when you become a child of God and the core of who you are is changed forever. This love ignites the centre of your being. Sparks a new dimension to your character. Transforms your personality. Makes you, at last, truly human.

The sons of God are the peacemakers. And the peacemakers are truly the sons of God.

We need peacemakers everywhere.

8

Blessed are those who are persecuted because of righteousness, for theirs is the kingdom of heaven

THE SHEEP AND THE LAMB

As Jesus gazed out over the wilderness He saw hundreds of sheep scattered across the lush green hills by the Sea of Galilee. Like all sheep, they were vulnerable. Exposed. Helpless. Powerless to ward off the hungry wolves that prowled across the isolated landscape.

These sheep reminded Him of His sheep. The little ones who followed Him and to whom He was the Good Shepherd. And all across the world He could see that these sheep, the sheep of His flock, were threatened and hunted. Innocent victims in a wicked evil world.

These faithful followers of His, the sheep who knew Him and whom He knew, were persecuted for their right-eousness. Their goodness. Their purity. Their wide-eyed innocence in a world of dark corruption.

Jesus looked beyond the constraints of time and space and surveyed His flock down all the centuries. And, as He watched, He saw that in every age His sheep were persecuted and in every place they knew the same kind of suffering.

Some of them were accused by false witnesses in mock trials. Others languished in lonely prison cells. Some endured physical torture by evil guards, while others tasted the bitter chalice of martyrdom itself.

But there were millions more whose persecution was more subtle. They walked a lonely path of **emotional torment**. They were **criticised**, **condemned** and **marginalised** in a world that despised their certainty.

Whatever form it took, however, this persecution was an evil force. It came with a power to break the spirit and a venom to corrupt the soul. As Jesus surveyed His flock across the generations He saw that they were persecuted everywhere.

His followers were persecuted in nations with so-called freedom and in countries ruled by martial law. In cities with free presses and in states with corrupt judges. In the whispered gossip of cocktail parties and in the violent disorder of unruly slums.

Jesus knew that persecution like this was the raw cost of following Him, the price for sharing His life. For just as the Good Shepherd suffered, so did His sheep. And all who would be part of His flock would fall victim to it, whoever they were and wherever they lived.

For the One they followed was not only the Shepherd who cared for His sheep – He was the sacrificial Lamb who gave His life for love.

SHEEP AND WOLVES

The rising tide of hatred for Jesus' flock was only to be expected. His followers would always stand out from the rest for they lived a different life.

Their poverty of spirit set them against the materialism of this transient age. Their mourning put them at odds with the hedonistic party culture of the day.

Their **meekness** took them to the back of the queue. Their hunger and thirst for **righteousness** made them contrary to the flow of the world's culture. It made them **unpopular** with the **popular**.

Their merciful way of living didn't endear them to the harsh economic realities of the business world. They could never succeed in organisations looking for employees with cold hearts and callous minds.

Their purity made them out of place in a world where anything goes. They seemed old-fashioned and politically incorrect to a society formed by pop culture ideology.

Their peacemaking was resented by both sides so they had to live in a no-man's-land where no one trusted them. They were strangers in their own back yard. Little wonder, then, that the sheep of His flock seemed out of place. Ripe for persecution.

Their righteousness set them at odds with the world. Their morality made others feel uncomfortable. Their virtue made them look peculiar. Their integrity made them stand out from the crowd. Their sheer goodness got up people's noses.

His flock were like sheep among wolves.

Sheep among wolves.

THE GOOD SHEPHERD

But still the Good Shepherd called His followers to walk this difficult path and they knew the authentic ring of His voice. It was a difficult road to travel, but He travelled it with them. And, where the way was impossible, He carried them.

The Good Shepherd cared for His sheep with a love beyond their understanding and He bore deep wounds in His hands and side to prove it. Such was the cost.

These little ones, though despised, continually made the world a better place. They were the **salt** that **purified** and **cleansed it**. They were a healing influence wherever they were to be found.

They were the light that lit up a world shot through with darkness. They were the scraps of leaven which made the dough rise and whose small contribution made everything better.

His flock was small. Weak. Outnumbered. Ill-equipped. But chosen to win a victory far beyond their own capability.

Their suffering was not the end of their story. Their daily rejection was not the final page. Their persecution did not rob them of their inheritance. For one day they would see all things put right.

At last, on Judgment Day the truth was out. Their lives had not been lived in vain. They had made a difference. The contribution of these little ones was greater than they'd ever known.

And, there, on the Holy Mountain, they saw the final judgment. The Good Shepherd separated His sheep from the goats.

At last the little ones who had lived the kingdom of heaven in the kingdoms of earth were honoured. The ones who had followed the Good Shepherd, while everyone else went the way of the world, were exalted. For He knew that their lives had been full of kindness and their deeds full of love. It had not all been a waste of time.

His flock had lived their lives with a kind of compassion which marked them out as different. Their view of things had been forged by their perspective from a higher place. Their eyes were fixed on a new tomorrow and their feet were set toward the green pasture of Eternal Home. And now, at last, they received their reward.

For they had reached the timeless place of the Eternal Here and Now. The paradise where His sheep find green pastures of fulfilment and the bliss of safe lodging. They were gathered round their Shepherd for eternity.

As they **bathed** in the River of Life the scars of all the painful years were healed in **cleansing love**. Their suffering was purged with the stream of new beginnings. Their rejection was washed away by the flow of **endless grace**.

And here, at last, was the end of their journey. Suffering and death had passed away and there would be no more tears.

They had reached the kingdom of heaven, the Eternal Here and Now.

The timeless place of the Eternal Here and Now.

Other titles by Rob Frost

Big Questions

Conversation Starters

Break Me, Shape Me

Go for Growth

Visions

Breaking Bread

People at Work

Pilgrims

Gospel End

Broken Cross

Burning Questions

When I Can't Pray

Thinking Clearly About God and Science

Which Way for the Church

Hopes and Dreams

A New Start

Jesus in the Third Millennium

Sharing Jesus in a New Millennium

A Closer Look at New Age Spirituality

National Distributors

UK: (and countries not listed below)
CWR, Waverley Abbey House, Waverley Lane, Farnham, Surrey GU9 8EP.
Tel: (01252) 784710 Outside UK (44) 1252 784710

AUSTRALIA: CMC Australasia, PO Box 519, Belmont, Victoria 3216.
Tel: (03) 5241 3288

CANADA: CMC Distribution Ltd, PO Box 7000, Niagara on the Lake, Ontario L0S 1JO.
Tel: 1800 325 1297

GHANA: Challenge Enterprises of Ghana, PO Box 5723, Accra.
Tel: (021) 222437/223249 Fax: (021) 226227

HONG KONG: Cross Communications Ltd, 1/F, 562A Nathan Road, Kowloon.
Tel: 2780 1188 Fax: 2770 6229

INDIA: Crystal Communications, 10-3-18/4/1, East Marredpally, Secunderabad – 500 026.
Tel/Fax: (040) 7732801

KENYA: Keswick Bookshop, PO Box 10242, Nairobi.
Tel: (02) 331692/226047 Fax: (02) 728557

MALAYSIA: Salvation Book Centre (M) Sdn Bhd, 23 Jalan SS 2/64,
47300 Petaling Jaya, Selangor.
Tel: (03) 78766411/78766797 Fax: (03) 78757066/78756360

NEW ZEALAND: CMC Australasia, PO Box 36015, Lower Hutt.
Tel: 0800 449 408 Fax: 0800 449 049

NIGERIA: FBFM, Helen Baugh House, 96 St Finbarr's College Road, Akoka, Lagos.
Tel: (01) 7747429/4700218/825775/827264

PHILIPPINES: OMF Literature Inc, 776 Boni Avenue, Mandaluyong City.
Tel: (02) 531 2183 Fax: (02) 531 1960

REPUBLIC OF IRELAND: Scripture Union, 40 Talbot Street, Dublin 1.
Tel: (01) 8363764

SINGAPORE: Armour Publishing Pte Ltd, Block 203A Henderson Road,
11–06 Henderson Industrial Park, Singapore 159546.
Tel: 276 9976 Fax: 276 7564

SOUTH AFRICA: Struik Christian Books, 80 MacKenzie Street,
PO Box 1144, Cape Town 8000.
Tel: (021) 462 4360 Fax: (021) 461 3612

SRI LANKA: Christombu Books, 27 Hospital Street, Colombo 1.
Tel: (01) 433142/328909

TANZANIA: CLC Christian Book Centre, PO Box 1384, Mkwepu Street, Dar es Salaam.
Tel/Fax (022) 2119439

USA: CMC Distribution, PO Box 644, Lewiston, New York, 14092-0644.
Tel: 1800 325 1297

ZIMBABWE: Word of Life Books, Shop 4, Memorial Building,
35 S Machel Avenue, Harare.
Tel: (04) 781305 Fax: (04) 774739

For email addresses, visit the CWR website: www.cwr.org.uk

Trusted
All Over the World

Daily Devotionals

    Books and Videos

Day and Residential Courses

    Counselling Training

Biblical Study Courses

    Regional Seminars

Ministry to Women

CWR have been providing training and resources for Christians since the 1960s. From our headquarters at Waverley Abbey House we have been serving God's people with a vision to help apply God's Word to everyday life and relationships. The daily devotional *Every Day with Jesus* is read by over half-a-million people in more than 150 countries, and our unique courses in biblical studies and pastoral care are respected all over the world.

For a free brochure about our seminars and courses or a catalogue of CWR resources please contact us at the following address.

CWR,
Waverley Abbey House,
Waverley Lane,
Farnham,
Surrey GU9 8EP

Telephone: 01252 784700
Email: mail@cwr.org.uk
Website: www.cwr.org.uk

 CRUSADE FOR WORLD REVIVAL   *Applying God's Word to everyday life and relationships*

Great Ways to Share Your Faith

This new series from Selwyn Hughes offers intelligent,
honest perspectives on life, faith and God for those in search
of answers to the big questions. A wonderful resource for
friendship evangelism that will encourage anyone searching
for God.

CAN I REALLY KNOW GOD?
ISBN 1-85345-234-3

* Is God there?
* Can I have a relationship with God?
* What can I do to really know God?

CAN I REALLY KNOW FULFILMENT?
ISBN 1-85345-235-1

* Is happiness really possible?
* Why won't the pain go away?
* Doesn't death end it all?
* What is the answer?